W9-CGP-775

Getting To Know...

Nature's Children

BISON

Laima Dingwall

Grolier

Facts in Brief

Classification of the North American Bison

Class: *Mammalia* (mammals)
Order: *Artiodactyla* (cloven-hoofed mammals)
Family: *Bovidae* (bovid family)
Genus: *Bison*
Species: *Bison bison*

World distribution. Exclusive to North America; closely related species (*Bison bonasus*) found only in Poland.

Habitat. Prairies, or forested and mountainous areas.

Distinctive physical characteristics. Shaggy hair around head and neck; high hump at shoulders; beard; short, up-curved horns.

Habits. Lives in roaming herds comprised of small bands, each led by older male; seasonal location shifts; agile and fast, good swimmer.

Diet. Mostly grasses, but also lichens, vetches, horsetails, and berries.

Edited by: Elizabeth Grace Zuraw
Design/Photo Editor: Nancy Norton
Photo Rights: Ivy Images

ISBN: 0-7172-8729-7

Have you ever wondered . . .

Meet the most magnificent animal in North America. It is the mighty bison—or buffalo, as it often is mistakenly called.

The bison is the largest land animal on this continent. It's also as much a part of the Old West as Jesse James and Buffalo Bill. This powerful animal is even mentioned in an old song that begins, "Oh, give me a home where the buffalo roam...." The song is called "Home on the Range." And that's exactly where most bison make their home.

Let's find out more about this legendary creature of the American plains.

The bison has a huge head that appears even bigger because of the long hair on its head and shoulders.

Playtime

Young bison love to play. They kick up their back legs and bound across fields in a bison version of tag, or they butt heads and shove each other in a pretend battle. Sometimes a young bison might even play-fight with a springy tree branch. It shoves the branch away with its head, only to have it bounce back again for another shove.

This play has a serious side. As they frolic, the young bison are strengthening their muscles and learning the skills they'll need to defend themselves and be part of a *herd,* a group of animals that stays together.

Playful young bison butt heads as they engage in a pretend battle.

Meet The Relatives

If the bison had a family reunion for all its North American relatives, who would come? Its cousins, of course: the Mountain Goat, Muskox, Bighorn Sheep, and Dall's Sheep.

All these animals have a number of things in common. They all chew *cud,* or undigested food. This means that these animals eat now and chew later, when they have more time. The bison and its relatives also have split hoofs for feet and horns on their heads. And none of these animals has any top front teeth.

Many people call the bison a buffalo. But that's not correct. Buffalo live in Asia and Africa, and they are only distantly related to bison. Buffalo and bison are different in two ways. Bison have a huge hump on their back; buffalo don't. And bison have 14 pairs of ribs; buffalo have 13 pairs.

Among the bison's relatives are muskoxen (shown here), animals that live in northern Canada and other Arctic regions. Like bison, they have shaggy beards, horns, a shoulder hump, and split hoofs.

Here a Bison, There a Bison

There are two types of bison in North America: the Wood Bison and the Plains Bison. It's fairly easy to tell the two apart. The Wood Bison is larger and it has a much darker and woollier coat than its cousin. And as you may have guessed from its name, the Wood Bison lives in wooded areas. For the most part, these wooded areas are farther north than the open plains where the Plains Bison live.

Opposite page: Wood Bison, larger and taller than Plains Bison, are the last of the truly wild bison.

Big, Bigger, Biggest

The bison is the biggest land animal in North America. A full-grown male Wood Bison stands between 5 and 6 1/2 feet (1 1/2 and 2 meters) tall at the shoulder—about the same height as an adult man. But unlike a man, a bison tips the scale at between 1,400 and 2,200 pounds (635 and 1,000 kilograms). That's about the same weight as 10 adult men put together! Female bison are slightly smaller.

Warm, Shaggy Coats

The bison's head, hump, and forelegs are covered with thick, shaggy, chocolate-brown fur. This fur coat is two coats in one. Close to the bison's body is a layer of thick *underfur,* which traps body-warmed air next to the bison's skin. Another coat of long, coarse, outer hairs, called *guard hairs,* sheds water and keeps out wind.

In spring, the bison gets ready for the hot weather ahead by shedding its warm winter coat. Its lighter summer coat takes about two months to grow in.

The bison's hindquarters and legs are covered with shorter, straight, coppery-brown fur. And a long thick beard grows from the bison's chin.

These bison have yet to shed the last few patches of their winter fur coat.

Hear, See, and Smell

You would have to be very clever—or lucky—to sneak up on a bison. The bison's round fuzzy ears can hear twigs crackle and snap some 500 feet (150 meters) away. Its big, soft brown eyes can spot something move up to half a mile (three-quarters of a kilometer) away. And its wide, flat nose can detect a scent up to 1 mile (1 1/2 kilometers) away.

Keen senses are particularly important to the Plains Bison. On the open range, they must be able to sense danger quickly because they have no place to hide from their enemies. Their only protection is to turn and fight or run away.

The thick fur on the front half of a bison's body gives so much cold weather protection that the animal always faces into a winter storm. Most other animals turn their backs on a blizzard of driving snow.

Horn Headgear

Both male and female bison have horns, but those of the male are larger. Bison use their horns to defend themselves against enemies, and males use theirs in fights with other bison.

Bison horns are very sharp and very long. A full-grown male may have horns as long as 15 inches (38 centimeters) each. To keep its horns sharp and polished, a bison rubs them against trees. If there are no trees nearby, it uses anything that sticks up from the ground: a boulder, a bush, or a sapling. Even a mound of dirt or a pile of snow in winter will do.

Bison have horns similar to those of domestic cattle. Some sets of bison horns can have an overall spread of as much as 35 inches (89 centimeters).

A Relaxing Rub

The bison rubs not only its horns against things, it also gets its head, shoulders, and sides into the rubbing act. At times, especially during the spring and summer when the bison has shed its winter coat, it seems to go rub crazy. No wonder. That's the time of year when biting insects are at their worst. Rubbing not only helps stop insect pests from biting, it also keeps them from laying their eggs on the bison's back.

To get their backs rubbed, sometimes bison even roll around on the ground. When this happens, dust flies everywhere as the animal flops back and forth. As the bison rolls around, a bowl-shaped hole is flattened out in the dust. These holes, called *wallows,* sometimes are 15 feet (4 1/2 meters) across.

Besides getting rid of insects, wallowing also helps bison rub off any loose patches of their winter fur coat. And now some scientists think that wallowing might also be the bison's way of relaxing and getting rid of tension.

Opposite page: *Clouds of dust rise as a bison enjoys a vigorous wallow.*

Tail End

At the end of a bison's tail is a tassle of long hair that makes a very good fly swatter. When the bison swishes its tail back and forth, it discourages flies and other insects from biting or laying their eggs on its hindquarters.

At rest

If you want to know what a bison is thinking, look at its tail. When the bison's tail is hanging down, the bison is calm. But when its tail is sticking up into the air, beware—it means that the bison is upset and may even charge.

Getting Around

Don't be fooled by the bison's bulky body. It can run as fast as a car moves on a city street—for short distances. The bison is also a fine swimmer. It's comfortable in water and swims dog-paddle style.

Alarmed

The bison is well equipped for mountain climbing, too. With its sharp hoofs and strong legs, it can easily handle rocky terrains.

Most bison have a life expectancy of about 20 years.

Bison on the Move

People once thought that bison spent the spring and summer grazing in the northern parts of their range, then migrated as far south as Texas to winter feeding grounds.

Today we know that bison seldom travel more than 200 miles (320 kilometers) during their *migration*, the regular annual trips bison make in search of food. The bison that spend their summers feeding on open plains travel to wooded areas in winter. Those that summer on mountains climb down into the valleys. There they find shelter among the trees and are protected from the worst of winter's icy storms.

Bison can run fast, but only for short distances.

Group Lunch

What do bison eat? Most of their diet is made up of grasses such as wild oats, wild rye, wheat, speargrass, and horsetails, which are plants related to ferns. They also eat lichens, vetches, blueberries, and bearberries.

Bison usually start to feed in early morning and munch away until dusk. They move around in a herd as they eat, keeping their muzzles close to the ground and tearing off tasty mouthfuls of grass.

Bison don't waste time chewing their food as they *graze,* or feed on growing grass. Instead, they store unchewed food in a special part of their stomach. When a bison has finished grazing, it looks for a resting spot, preferably out of the hot sun or cold winter winds. There it brings the unchewed food, or cud, back into its mouth and chews it in peace. Some bison chew their cud standing up, while others prefer to lie down and chew, chew, chew.

Snowplow Nose

In winter, the grass that the bison feeds on is covered by deep snow. But the bison is especially equipped to deal with this problem. It uses its large, flat nose as a built-in plow to shovel away the snow and uncover the grass. The bison pushes its nose through the snow, stopping at times to swing its head back and forth to sweep away the snow. The bison's snowplow nose is so effective that it can push away piles of snow more than 3 feet (1 meter) deep.

Powerful heads and large noses make easy work of bison snow removal.

Home on the Range

At one time, there were about 60 million bison in North America. There were so many that if they lined up in twos and walked past you, one pair every minute, the parade would last almost 60 years! All these bison made their home on the central plains of North America. They lived as far north as Great Slave Lake in Canada's Northwest Territories and as far south as Mexico.

By 1900, these vast herds of bison were almost wiped out. Only a few hundred were left in all of North America. What happened to this once-bountiful inhabitant of the plains?

The huge herds of bison that once roamed America created trails that were the best routes through mountains and plains. Later when people built highways, many of the roads followed those well-worn bison paths.

For centuries, the Plains Indians of North America had hunted the bison. But they hunted with spears, killing relatively few of the animal. And they made use of every part of it: They used the hides to make tents and clothes, the meat for food, and the horns and bones to make tools.

But once European settlers came to North America, things changed very quickly. The settlers brought guns, which made it very easy to kill the bison. Soon there were almost no bison left in North America.

Bison often take an afternoon nap.

The Bison Come Back

By the early 1900s, people started to realize that hunting for bison should be stopped, or soon even the few hundred remaining animals would be gone. As a result, concerned people created national parks where hunting bison was not permitted. Gradually, the animal's numbers increased. Today, some 50,000 bison live in national parks, on game preserves, and on private ranches scattered across the western *prairies,* large areas of mostly flat, rolling, and treeless grasslands.

Opposite page: A full-grown bison is so strong that it can run through a fence and could even overturn a car, let alone fend off an attacker.

Enemy List

Before the early settlers came to North America, the main enemies of the bison were the Grizzly Bear, the Mountain Lion and the wolf. But these *predators,* animals that hunt other animals for food, usually attack only the very young or very old and sick bison. They seldom go after healthy adults. And for good reason. A bison has large hoofs and sharp horns to defend itself.

33

The More the Merrier

A lone bison is an unhappy bison. That's because the bison is a very social animal. It likes to live and travel with other bison in a herd, seeming to know that there is safety in numbers. An enemy, such as a wolf, might be tempted to attack a single bison, but not a whole herd. Usually bison travel together in small groups of about 20. These small groups then sometimes get together to make a large herd. A herd can be made up of as many as 1,000 bison.

Bison in a group usually do the same thing at the same time. When one bison wakes up at dawn and starts to graze, soon all the other bison in the herd begin to graze, too. And when one bison lies down to chew its cud, the others soon follow suit. In a while the entire herd is chewing.

Once numbering in the tens of millions, by 1900 only about 300 bison were left in the United States. Efforts to save the bison have kept the animal from extinction, *or going out of existence.*

Stampede

Sometimes an odd noise frightens a bison. Then it might get nervous and start to run. Soon, all the other bison in the herd are racing around, too. This momentary madness and confused rush is called a *stampede*.

Stampedes can be very dangerous. Often the animals at the front of the stampede can't stop or turn aside when they come upon an obstacle. If they stumble and fall, they are trampled by the bison behind them. Native Americans sometimes used the stampede as a way of hunting bison. They would deliberately start a stampede and force the bison to run over a cliff and jump to their deaths. That way the hunters could catch many bison at one time.

In North America today, some places where herds of bison live are Custer State Park (SD), Badlands National Monument (ND), National Bison Range (MT), Wichita Mountains Refuge (OK), and Yellowstone National Park (WY). The largest herd is in Wood Buffalo National Park in Alberta, Canada.

Mating Time

Bison *mate,* or come together to produce young, in late summer and early fall. At that time, small groups of male bison, or *bulls,* join a large herd of female bison, or *cows.*

Once a bull finds a mate, he usually bellows like a foghorn in hopes of frightening away any rivals. Any bull foolhardy enough to ignore this loud warning is usually charged. When this happens, the two bulls rush toward each other until they collide. They often hit with such a powerful force that dust and dirt fly from their fur. Fortunately, few of the animals ever get hurt. The shaggy mane of hair on top of a bison's head softens the blows.

Sometimes when two bulls charge at one another, they lock horns and have a shoving match, pushing each other back and forth. The winner of the match usually wins the female.

Bison are ready to mate at about three years of age. Though both have grown large, females are smaller and less shaggy than males.

A Baby is Born

In early summer, when food is plentiful, the cow gives birth. She often wanders a short distance from her herd and picks a quiet spot—usually in a clump of trees—as her nursery. There, she gives birth to one baby bison, or *calf.* Sometimes twins are born, but this is rare.

The newborn baby bison looks much like a baby cow, except that it is much stockier and its neck is shorter. Its eyes and ears are open, and its body is already covered with a fuzzy orange-colored coat.

Calves are a light tawny color, in contrast to the dark brown of their parents.

Mother and Baby

The mother bison licks her baby very carefully as soon as it is born. Within minutes, the baby tries to stand up. Its legs are still weak and wobbly, and it usually collapses into a sprawling heap. But the baby tries again, and within about half an hour it is standing up by itself. In a few hours the baby may even be running in circles around its mother.

For the first two or three days of its life, the calf stays close to its mother—away from the rest of the herd. It spends all its time sleeping and *nursing,* drinking milk from its mother's body. Even when mother and baby join the herd, the two are never far apart. But within a couple of weeks, the calf begins to play with the other calves in the herd. Soon it is spending most of the time with these young bison and visits its mother only once in a while to nurse.

A mother bison usually has only one calf at a time, born about nine months after she has mated.

Big Babies

Opposite page:
A young bison's coat won't change to a dark chocolate-brown until it is about 14 weeks old.

Even though a bison calf drinks its mother's milk until it is seven months old, it starts to nibble grass when it is only one week old. With all this eating and playful exercise, the calf grows quickly.

By the time it is six weeks old, the bison calf is strong enough to knock a full-grown man off his feet. At eight weeks of age, the hump on its back and its horns start to grow. At first the horns are only tiny furred bumps. These don't reach adult size until the bison is eight years old.

By ten weeks, the young bison's high-pitched baby squeal changes to a low, deep, grunty voice, and its fur begins to grow darker.

The young bison now starts spending most of its time with the other young bison and little time with its mother. In fact, young bison can often be found playing, grazing, and sleeping together in the middle of the herd, while the adult bison stay on the outside.

Happy Birthday

By the time a young bison celebrates its first birthday, it weighs 400 pounds (180 kilograms) and its horns are 7 inches (17 centimeters) long. The time has come for the young bison to leave its mother. If it's a male, it will join the other males in a small group. If it's a female, it will become part of the big herd.

In about three years, the bison will be ready to mate, even though it won't become a full-grown adult until it is about eight years old. Some bison in the wild have lived to be 40 years old, but most live only to about 20. During that time a bison will have several families, and its children and grandchildren will become part of the herd, too.

Words To Know

Bull   A male bison.

Calf   A baby bison.

Cow   A female bison.

Cud   Hastily swallowed food brought back for chewing at a later time. Cud chewers include deer, cows, and bison.

Extinction   Going out of existence.

Graze   To feed on growing grass.

Guard hairs   Long coarse hairs that make up the outer layer of a bison's coat.

Herd   Group of animals that stays together.

Hoofs   Feet of cattle, deer, bison, and some other animals.

Mate   To come together to produce young.

Migration   The regular annual trips animals make in search of food.

Nurse   To drink milk from a mother's body.

Prairie   A large area of mostly flat, rolling, and treeless grasslands.

Predator   Animal that hunts other animals for food.

Range   Area that the bison lives in.

Stampede   A wild rush of frightened or confused animals.

Underfur   Short, dense hair that traps body-warmed air next to an animal's skin.

Wallow   The hollowed-out area created when a bison rolls on the ground, or rolling around in such a hollow.

Index

PHOTO CREDITS
Cover: J. D. Markou, *Valan Photos.* **Interiors:** Maslowski Photo, 4, 28. */Ivy Images:* Lynn & Donna Rogers, 6-7, 40; Robert McCaw, 18; Don Johnston, 21, 26. */Canada In Stock / Ivy Images:* Mike Beedell, 9; Brian Hay, 10, 12-13; Gary Crandall, 17, 39. */Valan Photos:* Wayne Lankinen, 14; Stephen J. Krasemann, 24; Hälle Flygare, 31; Thomas Kitchin, 32; Dennis Schmidt, 36; J. D. Markou, 42. */Hot Shots / Ivy Images:* J. D. Taylor, 22-23. */Parks Canada Photo Services,* 35. */Barry Ranford,* 45.

Getting To Know...

Nature's Children

OPOSSUM

Laima Dingwall

Grolier

Facts in Brief

Classification of the Opossum

    Class: *Mammalia* (mammals)

    Order: *Marsupialia* (marsupials)

    Family: *Didelphidae* (New World opossums)

    Genus: *Didelphis*

    Species: *Didelphis virginiana*

World distribution. Exclusive to North and South America. Other marsupials are found in South America and Australia.

Habitat. Woods, pastures, and parks. Prefers areas where water is available.

Distinctive physical characteristics. Fur-lined abdominal pouch on females; large thin black naked ears; long thin tail; large pink naked nose tip; white or black-tipped fur.

Habits. Most active at night; can both climb trees and swim; lives in the abandoned burrows of other animals; sometimes plays dead if captured by a predator; younger ones can hang upside down from tree branches by their tails.

Edited by: Elizabeth Grace Zuraw
Design/Photo Editor: Nancy Norton
Photo Rights: Ivy Images

ISBN: 0-7172-8729-7

Have you ever wondered . . .

If you have ever seen an opossum, you have seen one of the most unusual animals in North America. What is so remarkable about the opossum—or possum, as some people call it?

Well, to begin with, the opossum is the only animal in North America that hangs upside down by its tail. More than that, it has "hands" on its back legs, "feet" on its front legs, and the female carries her babies in a pouch on her abdomen, or belly. Read on to find out more about this shy and odd, but fascinating creature that likes to be left alone.

Long white hairs over a layer of black-tipped fur gives the opossum a silvery look.

Where's Mom?

Opossum babies are very attached to their mother. They spend their first six weeks of life in a warm furry *pouch,* or pocket, on her abdomen. In just a week's time, they grow to ten times their size at birth. When they grow too big to fit into the pouch, they climb out. But even after they leave the pouch for good, opossum babies like to be near their mother. Sometimes they even hitch a ride on her back when they get tired.

When young opossums are old enough to take care of themselves, they go off on their own. What is in store for them?

A baby opossum will grow to be about as big as a house cat.

Relatives Near and Far

If you could travel back 200 million years to the age of the dinosaurs, you would probably see the tiny opossum scurrying between the legs of the mighty Brontosaurus. Of course, there are no dinosaurs around today—but the opossum is still here.

The opossum belongs to an ancient group of animals called the *marsupials*. Besides being old-timers, marsupials have something else in common. The female carries her babies in a fur-lined pouch on her abdomen.

The common opossum, or Virginia Opossum, is the only marsupial that lives in North America. Scientists believe it traveled up from South America millions of years ago. Early Native Americans gave it the name we know today. They called it *apasum,* which means "white animal."

Several opossum relatives still live in Mexico and Central and South America, but perhaps the most famous marsupials of all live in Australia. They are the kangaroo, wallaby, wombat, Tasmanian devil, and koala.

Opposite page: *Long, sharp claws make the opossum an excellent tree climber.*

9

Opossum Country

Most North American opossums live in the warm southeastern parts of the United States. But in the last 100 years or so, opossums have started to move north into the New England states and southern Canada. And opossums can even be found as far west as California, Oregon, Washington, and southern British Columbia.

Opossums often live at the edge of a forest or on farmlands. They don't stray far from a stream or *marsh,* an area where the ground is soaked with water. Some opossums have even moved into suburbs, towns, and cities, where they usually set up home in parks.

Opossums often scoot up trees to escape from their enemies. They also like to sleep in the branches.

Sizing Up the Opossum

Imagine a white rat as big as a house cat. That's what the opossum looks like. A full-grown male opossum weighs as much as 12 pounds (6 kilograms), or about as much as a fat cat. From the tip of its nose to the end of its tail it measures 24 to 32 inches (60 to 80 centimeters). Female opossums are slightly smaller.

Opposite page:
The opossum is a nocturnal animal, it is active mainly at night.

Bless My Whiskers

An opossum has four rows of cat-like whiskers—each about 3 inches (8 centimeters) long—growing out from the sides of its nose and cheeks. And just like a cat's whiskers, the opossum's whiskers are sensitive feelers. This is especially useful when the opossum is wandering through brush at night in search of food. If it can get its head through a narrow opening without its whiskers touching the sides, then the opossum knows it can probably squeeze the rest of its body through, too.

Opossum Picnic

When it is hungry, the opossum keeps its round, pink nose close to the ground so that it can sniff out its dinner quickly. It will eat almost anything that flies, crawls, hops, or even walks by.

Its favorite foods are insects, especially crickets, grasshoppers, beetles, and butterflies. But it also eats small animals such as snails, earthworms, salamanders, frogs, and lizards. Even snakes are considered a tasty treat! An opossum on the prowl will raid birds' nests to feast on the eggs or young birds, and it also hunts mice, young rabbits, squirrels, and moles. In the city, the opossum often knocks over garbage cans and digs up vegetable gardens in its search for food.

An opossum isn't a fussy eater. It'll snack on just about anything.

14

The opossum also eats fruit and plants. It will gorge on berries and other fruit that have fallen to the ground, and if it's still hungry, it will climb trees in search of more. Opossums that live in the South particularly enjoy persimmons and pokeberries. And it's common to see them feeding on grasses, clover, seeds, and nuts.

If there's a lot of food available, an opossum's *home range,* the area where it lives, might be no bigger than 12 acres (5 hectares). But during lean times, the animal may wander over an area four times that size as it looks for food.

An apple or any other fruit is always a treat for an opossum.

Fuzzy Fur

Most of the opossum's body is covered with a double-thick fur coat. The white outer coat, made up of stiff, finger-length *guard hairs,* helps to keep the opossum dry. The inner coat of thick, short hair is warm and woolly. It traps in body heat. This inner coat can either be pure white or white tipped with black. The mixture of white and black fur gives the opossum its silvery gray color.

Like a cat, an opossum uses its rough tongue to *groom,* or clean, its coat. First it licks its front paws clean and uses them to scrub its face. Then it usually sits on its haunches and gives its belly a good cleaning.

An opossum licks its paws clean as it begins a session of grooming.

Double Grip

Imagine having your hands where your feet are and your feet where your hands are. That may sound backwards to you, but the opossum finds such an arrangement very useful.

The opossum has a thumb on each of its back paws. That means it can grip things the way you can with your hands. Having a thumb is a terrific help to a tree climber whose safety depends on hanging on. The opossum also has an extra "hand"—its tail. The tail can wrap around a branch while the opossum is high up in a tree, leaving its hands free to grab the next branch.

Getting up and down trees is no problem either. The opossum has long sharp claws on all of its fingers and toes, except its thumbs. It digs these claws into the tree bark for a good safe grip.

An opossum is well equipped to get a good grip on things. It even has a thumb on each of its back paws (inset photo).

Hanging Around

The opossum is the only animal in North America that can hang upside down by its tail. Some scientists believe that the animal originally developed the tail as a grasping tool for living in trees. The opossum's tail is known as a *prehensile,* or grasping, tail. It's easy to see how the opossum uses it. It simply wraps the tail around a tree branch and lets go with its hands.

If you see an opossum hanging upside down by its tail, it's probably a young opossum. Full-grown opossums are too large and heavy to hang by their tails, except for a very short period of time. If they tried it for any longer, they'd probably land headfirst on the ground!

An opossum's tail is long, scaly, and hairless—but very useful. It allows the animal to hang upside down from a branch, freeing its paws for other activity.

Opossum on the Run

If you ran a race against an opossum, who would win? Probably you would. The fastest time ever recorded for an opossum was only 8 miles (13 kilometers) an hour.

But even if you were to outrun an opossum, you probably wouldn't be able to catch it. The opossum is built so low to the ground that it can easily duck under bushes and shrubs, squeeze into small holes in the ground, scurry into hollow logs, hide behind piles of rocks, or even nip up a tree to avoid you.

A walking opossum is a real slowpoke. It has a plodding, awkward-looking gait because it moves the two legs on the same side of its body at the same time.

Opossums are very adept at finding good hiding places both on the ground and in trees.

Opossum Hideaway

Opossums don't spend a lot of time and energy digging a nest or building any other kind of home for themselves. Instead, they take over a burrow abandoned by a ground-hog or skunk, or just move into a hollow log or even the hollow of a tree. In the city, an opossum might make its home under a house porch, in a garage, or inside a storm sewer.

Once it has moved in, an opossum lines its den with plenty of leaves and twigs for comfort and warmth. How does the opossum carry this bedding to its home? First, it gathers leaves with its front feet and pushes them under its body. Then it wraps its long, flexible tail around the leaves, picks them up, and hurries home, carrying the load of leaves with its tail.

When its *den*, or animal home, is finished, the opossum snoozes away the days in it.

Seldom building a house for itself, an opossum prefers to take over a burrow abandoned by another animal.

Bundle Up!

The opossum is not built to withstand frosty weather. The bottoms of its feet are bare, and so are its long, thin ears. And except for a few stiff bristles, its tail is naked, too. This is not a problem for opossums that live in warm climates, but what about those that have moved into cold-weather country?

If the weather gets really cold, an opossum spends up to two weeks at a stretch snuggled up in its den. It does not go out to search for food. Instead it lives off a thick layer of body fat that it built up by eating a lot of food in the fall. But in a long cold spell, the opossum must go out and look for food. Brrr! Many northern opossums have lost the tips of their ears and the end of their tails because of frostbite.

During winter an opossum may have to risk frostbite in order to get a drink.

"Playing Possum"

Owls, foxes, and bobcats are just a few of the animals that consider opossums a tasty meal. To avoid these *predators,* animals that hunt other animals for food, an opossum often runs for a safe hiding spot. But because opossums are not fast runners, they've come up with another trick to fool their pursuers. The opossum flops over and plays dead! Since none of its enemies will eat a dead animal, the opossum often saves itself that way.

How does an opossum play dead—or "play possum," as it's usually called? When an enemy gets too close, the opossum topples over on its side, lets its mouth drop open, and often closes its eyes. It even slows down its breathing and heart rate. The opossum won't budge or flicker its eyes even if its enemy pokes at it or picks it up in its mouth and shakes it.

However, sometimes the opossum gets mixed up. If the predator puts it back on the ground upside down, the opossum may forget it's supposed to be dead. It flips over quite alive, onto its feet. So much for playing dead!

An Opossum Means Business

If an opossum is cornered by an enemy and doesn't have a chance to "play possum," it may try to frighten off the attacker. It faces its enemy, opens its mouth wide to show off its sharp teeth, and hisses and growls loudly.

The opossum even makes itself look bigger than it really is by standing up as tall as possible and holding its tail straight up. The sight of such a fierce-looking and determined animal is often enough to make most of its enemies think twice about attacking.

The opossum may be a small animal, but it can put up a good defense.

Mating Time

The opossum is a loner and usually chooses to live by itself. The only time that adult opossums can be seen together is during *mating season,* the time of year during which the animals come together to *mate,* or produce young. When an opossum mates depends on where it lives. Opossums that live in the South mate from January to August. More northerly opossums mate between February and August.

Opossums usually mate only once during the mating season. But sometimes a female opossum may mate twice and have two *litters,* or families of young born together, in one season—the first in late February and the second in late July.

Adult opossums come together only during mating season. An opossum is ready to start a family when it is about eight months old.

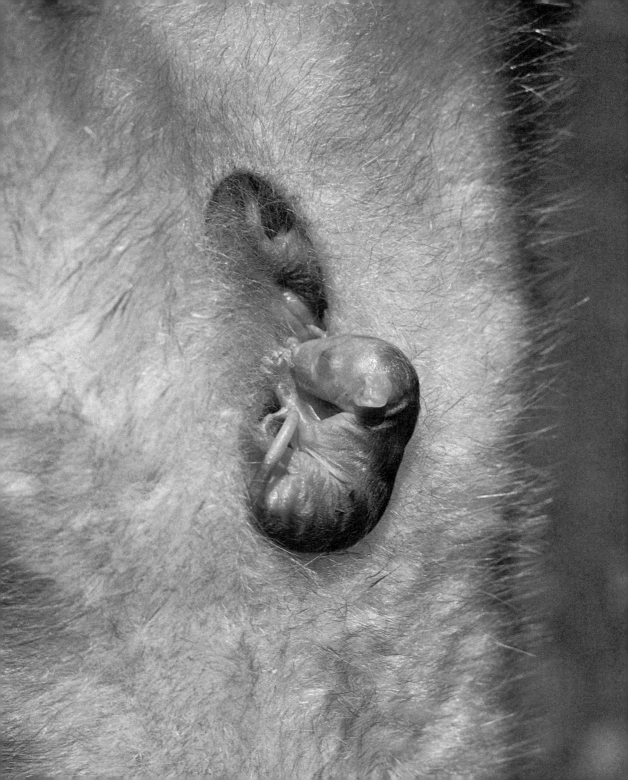

A Cozy Nursery

Just 13 days after mating, the female opossum is ready to give birth. She lines her den with plenty of leaves and twigs to make a cozy nursery. There she gives birth to as many as 20 babies at one time. She raises her babies alone, without any help from the male.

You could easily hold an entire litter of 20 opossums in a tablespoon! The newborn opossum measures just half an inch (14 millimeters) long from one end to the other. That's about the size of a honeybee.

The newborn opossum is rosy pink and hairless. Its ears and eyes are still closed and its back legs and tail are small stubs. But its front legs are well developed and come equipped with claws.

The opossum is a mammal: *It breathes air, is born alive, drinks its mother's milk, and has hair.*

Everyone into the Pouch, Please

The first few moments of a baby opossum's life are quite busy. As soon as it is born, the mother opossum licks it very carefully. Next she licks the fur on her abdomen to make it moist and slippery. The baby, using the tiny claws on its front feet as mini-hooks, wriggles and squirms its way along this slippery path until it finds the fur-lined pouch on its mother's belly. Then it crawls in.

With so many young, it can be quite a tight squeeze in a mother opossum's pouch.

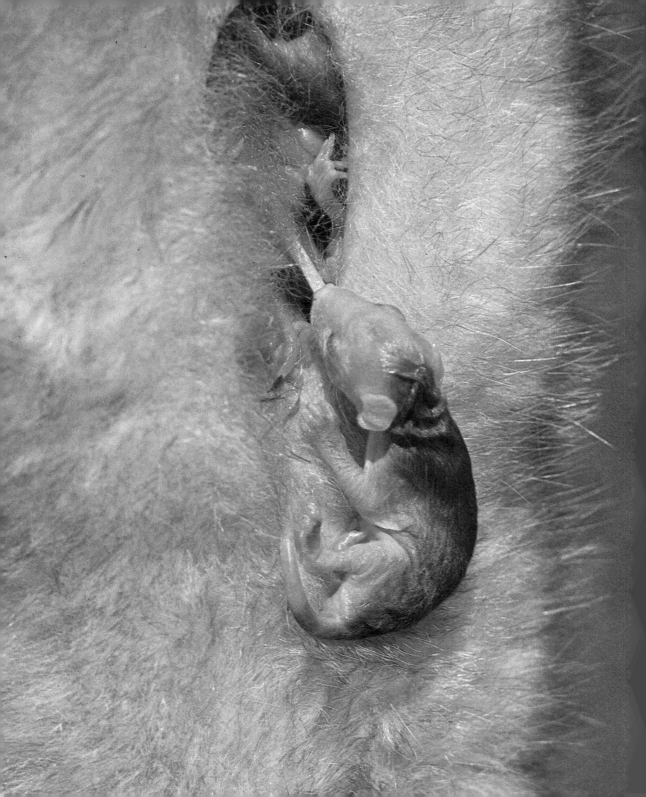

Home Sweet Pouch

The mother opossum's pouch is like a big, warm, woolly pocket. She can open her pocket whenever she likes by simply relaxing her muscles, and close it again by tightening them.

Hidden inside this pouch are 13 nipples arranged in the shape of a horseshoe. There are 12 nipples along the edge and one nipple in the center. A *nipple* is the part of the mother's body through which a baby drinks the mother's milk.

Even though the opossum mother sometimes gives birth to as many as 20 babies at once, she has only 13 nipples, so she can feed only 13 babies. There's one nipple for one baby. Those newborns that don't find a nipple don't survive.

Each newborn opossum struggles to latch onto one of its mother's nipples.

41

Growing Up Inside a Pouch

Once inside its mother's pouch, the newborn opossum finds a nipple and immediately starts to *nurse,* or drink its mother's rich milk. It will not let go of this nipple for about 60 days.

The baby grows very quickly, and life inside the pouch gets more and more crowded. About 14 days after birth, the baby starts to grow fuzzy, silvery fur. Its back legs and tail grow longer and stronger, and it gains weight steadily. But it is not until the baby opossum opens its eyes—between the ages of 58 and 72 days—that it becomes curious about the outside world. It is only then that it lets go of the nipple and finally pokes its head outside the pouch.

A young opossum has a life expectancy of about seven years.

Hello There, World!

Though it may be out of the pouch, the baby opossum is still weak and quite helpless. And although it starts to explore the world, it does not stray far from its mother. Because its legs are still rather wobbly, it often rides piggyback style, clinging with its tiny, but strong, claws to its mother's back.

Traveling this way, the mother takes all her babies out on short trips from the nest. During these outings, she shows them how to find food and climb trees.

A mother opossum is a busy creature. She carries her babies in her pouch for about two months. Then, after the babies leave her pouch, she carries them on her back until they are strong enough to get around on their own.

Moving Out

The baby opossum nurses until it is about 100 days old. When it is hungry, it just climbs into its mother's pouch and latches onto a nipple. Sometimes, if the mother is lying on her side sunning herself, the baby opossum hangs backwards out of the pouch and suns itself, too, without letting go of the nipple.

The baby opossum grows and learns quickly. By the time it is 100 days old, it is ready to leave its mother and find a den of its own. Usually it doesn't wander far from its mother's den. But although it lives nearby, the young opossum doesn't spend time with its mother or brothers and sisters. Now it prefers to be on its own. When it's about eight months old, it will be ready to mate and start a family of its own.

Words To Know

Den   Animal home.

Groom   To clean.

Guard hair   Long coarse hairs that make up the outer layer of an opossum's coat.

Home range   The area where an opossum lives and looks for food.

Litter   Young animals born together.

Mammal   A class of animals that breathes air, is warm-blooded, is born alive, drinks its mother's milk, and has hair at some stage of its life.

Marsh   An area where the ground is soaked with water.

Marsupials   A family of animals whose females carry their young in a pouch until they are fully developed.

Mate   To come together to produce young.

Mating season   The time of year during which animals mate.

Nipple   The part of the mother's body through which a baby drinks the mother's milk.

Nocturnal   Active mainly at night.

Nurse   To drink milk from a mother's body.

Pouch   The fur-lined pocket of a female marsupial where her babies live until they are developed.

Predator   An animal that lives by hunting other animals.

Prehensile   Used for grasping, especially by wrapping around.

Index

PHOTO CREDITS

Cover: Steve Maslowski. **Interiors:** Karl H. Maslowski, 4, 36, 39, 40. /Leonard Lee Rue III, 7, 21 (large photo), 43. /*Valan Photos:* R. C. Simpson, 8, 35. /Leonard Lee Rue IV, 11, 32. /H. R. Hungerford, 12. /*Ivy Images:* Robert McCaw, 15. /Steve Maslowski, 16, 19, 23, 24, 27, 28. /Wayne Lynch, 21 (inset). /Maslowski Photo, 31. /Len Rue Jr., 44.